A Roots Mbili Theatre and Sheffield Theatres co-production

FAR GONE

by John Rwothomack

Far Gone was first produced as a co-production between Roots Mbili Theatre & Sheffield Theatres at The Crucible Theatre, with support from Theatre Deli Sheffield, 2022.

Cast and Creative Team

Writer and Actor	**John Rwothomack**
Director	**Mojisola Elufowoju**
Producer	**Sam Holland**
Dramaturg	**Paul Sirett**
Sound Designer	**Lee Affen**
Lighting Designer	**Will Monks**
Set & Costume Designer	**Kevin Jenkins**
Movement Director	**Akeim Toussaint Buck**
Movement Director	**Lilac Yosiphon**
Stage & Tour Manager	**Hannah Birtwistle-Crossland**
Stage & Tour Manager	**Tori Klays**
Artwork & Photography	**Smart Banda**
Videographer	**Gomolemo Nyakale**

Biographies

John Rwothomack | Writer & Actor

John is a Ugandan-born, London-trained, and Sheffield-bred-and-based actor, director and playwright. He trained at Rose Bruford.

As an artist, John aims to bring African stories, culture and history to the canvas of theatre. This might include creating new pieces about, and with artists from the continent, staging plays that already exist, or adapting classics to an African context. John holds the view that African culture is not present enough in the UK's theatre scene. As a result, there's a lower rate of participation both in audience members and practitioners from this sector of the community.

As an actor, credits include: *H&P*, *On Missing* (The Cockpit Theatre, London, 2019); *Dr Bupe*, *Tales from the Playground* (Paper Finch Theatre, Sheffield, 2018); *Priest*, *The Devil In Mary* (Short Film, York, 2017); *Witch Doctor*, *The Emperor Jones* (The Lost Theatre, London, 2016); *John Blanke*, *The Low Road* (Stratford Circus, London, 2015).

As a director: *Bad Blood Blues* (Theatre Deli, 2018); *Ally* (short film, 2020).

As an assistant director: *The Last King of Scotland* (Sheffield Theatres, 2019); *White Noise* (Bridge Theatre, 2021).

Mojisola Elufowoju | Director

Mojisola Elufowoju is the CEO and Artistic Director of Utopia Theatre, a leading African theatre company resident at Sheffield Crucible Theatre.

She was staff director at the National Theatre, working on *Three Sisters* by Inua Ellams. She was a recipient of the 2017 Opera Awards Foundation bursary, a founding member of Mosaic Opera Collective, guest director at British American Drama Academy, East 15, London South Bank University and University of the West of Scotland.

She is passionate about the growth and development of ethnic minorities in the theatre industry. Her work is to raise awareness and increase appreciation of African culture. She commissions and produces new writing and presents established classics within a strong African context, and in so doing, dispelling stereotypes and encouraging authentic voices from the African diaspora.

Credits include: *Here's What She Said To Me* (Utopia Theatre/Sheffield Crucible); *How Far Apart?* (Utopia Theatre at Arcola Theatre and Sheffield Hallam Performance Lab); *Far Gone* (Theatre Deli – Sheffield and Sheffield Theatre Studio); *The Bogus Woman* (London South Bank University at Camden People's Theatre); *On Missing* (Wretched Theatre at The Cockpit Theatre); *Shadows in Different Shades* (Utopia Theatre at Sheffield Theatre Studio); *The Pied Piper of Chibok Opera* (Utopia Theatre at Opera North and Arcola Theatre); *I am David Oluwale* (Utopia Theatre at Leeds Playhouse); *Iyalode of Eti* (Utopia Theatre at Leeds Playhouse, Sheffield Crucible, Cast – Doncaster and Ake Festival Nigeria); *London Tales* (Utopia Theatre at Rich Mix and Lost Theatre); *This Is Our Chance* (James Ene Henshaw Foundation at Cultural Centre Calabar, Nigeria); *The Shepherd's Chameleon* (Utopia Theatre at CLF Art Cafe); *House of Corrections* (Riverside Studios); *Wake Me When It's Time* (York Theatre Royal).

Sam Holland | Producer

Sam is a Sheffield-based freelance theatre producer and festival director.

He has run the UK's largest Refugee Week festival, Migration Matters Festival in Sheffield since 2016 and project-managed the inaugural SoAfrica Festival in 2018.

Having first worked with John Rwothomack on *Bad Blood Blues* in 2018, Sam has produced *Far Gone* since 2019, helping take the show to Kampala before the 2020 pandemic. Other credits include: *Benny and the Greycats* (Maya Productions); *My Name is Rachel Corrie*, 2019; *The Pianist of Sarajevo*, 2021 and *There Is No Planet B*, 2021 (all with Hassun El Zafar).

In 2021 he started 'Creative Journeys', a mentorship programme providing aspiring artists from marginalised backgrounds, support and expert guidance in refining and pursuing their craft.

Paul Sirett | Dramaturg

Paul is a dramaturg, playwright and musician.

As a dramaturg, Paul has worked on productions for numerous companies including the Ambassador Theatre Group, the Royal Shakespeare Company, and Soho Theatre Company. Paul recently adapted The Who's *Tommy* for d/Deaf and disabled actors (Ramps on the Moon, UK tour, 2017).

As a playwright, Paul has over twenty productions to his name including the Olivier-nominated musical, *The Big Life*. Recent productions include *Clear White Light* (Live Theatre, 2018); *Oxy and the Morons* (New Wolsey Theatre, 2017) and *Reasons to be Cheerful* (Graeae, 2017).

Kevin Jenkins | Designer

Kevin has been designing for theatre for 12 years after training on the Motley Theatre Design Course.

He has designed for Alan Ayckbourn in both Scarborough and New York. Productions include *The Girl Next Door*, *Season's Greetings*, *Birthdays Past Birthdays Present*, *Taking Steps* and *A Brief History of Women*.

Productions for Sheffield Theatres include *Songs from the Seven Hills*, *What We Wished For*, *A Dream*, *Hospital Food*, *The Beauty Inspector*, *Confessions of a City*, *Warrior Square*, *Topdog/Underdog* and *Hearts*. *Hearts* went on to be performed at the National Theatre.

Other theatre work includes: *Coram Boy* (Nottingham Playhouse); *The Frontline* (Curve); *The Last Seam* (Cast, Doncaster); *Shiv* (Curve); *1936* (Lilian Baylis Studio, Arcola Theatre); *Jane Hair* (Buglight Theatre Co); *Troublesome People* (Ashrow Theatre Co); *Abigail's Party* (Stantonbury Theatre); *Hamlet* (Blue Apple Theatre Co); *Colony* (Dark Horse); *The Pendulum* (Jermyn Street); *200 Years* (Watford Palace Theatre); *A Wedding Story* (Tristan Bates Theatre) and *Sonata* (Tara Arts).

Kevin has designed opera sets for Co-Opera Co's productions of *Albert Herring*, La bohème, *Carmen*, *The Marriage of Figaro* and *The Magic Flute*.

Will Monks | Lighting Designer

Will is a London-based lighting and video designer; he trained at Bristol Old Vic Theatre School.

Recent theatre work includes: *Foxes* (Theatre503); *I Stand For What I Stand On* (national tour); *The Great Big Story Mix Up* (Digital); *Sunnymead Court* (The Actors Centre and Digital, nominated for 4 Offie Awards); *I, Cinna (the poet)* (Unicorn Theatre, Digital; Winner of Theatre for Young People 12+ OnComm Award); *The Glass Will Shatter* (Omnibus Theatre); *Ali & Dahlia* (Pleasance London; nominated for Best Video Designer: Offie Award); *Trojan Horse* (UK tour, Edinburgh; winner of Fringe First and Amnesty International Freedom of Expression Awards); *Jericho's Rose* (Hope Theatre); *The Snow Queen, Pinocchio* (Old Rep Theatre); *The Dark Room* (Theatre503; nominated for Best Lighting Designer: Offie Award); *Who Cares* (winner of Sit-Up Award); *We Live By The Sea* (nominated for Best Ensemble and Best Production: Offie Awards); *This Is Where We Live* (international tours); *The Benidorm Elvis Fiesta* (Benidorm Palace); *Chilcot* (The Lowry, Battersea Arts Centre).

Lee Affen | Sound Designer

Lee is a multi-instrumentalist composer, music producer and sound designer from Manchester, now based in Sheffield. His passion for music and collaboration has led him to work in bands, write for singers and compose for theatre, dance and film. Lee is a company member of The Bare Project, an Associate artist with Imagine If Theatre and also Box of Tricks Theatre.

Lee's credits include: *Who Are Yer?* (Cardboard Citizens); *Jadek* and *My Old Man* (Imagine If); *The War Within* (Fallen Angels and Birmingham Royal Ballet); *Far Gone* (Roots Mbili – BBC Radio 3 and New Voices); *Outskirts* (The Bare Project); *Anna Hibiscus' Song* (Utopia Theatre and The Blahs); *Where Two Rivers Meet* (The British Library); *Hansel and Gretel: The Fairytale Detectives* (Paperfinch Theatre and Theatre Clwyd); *Ladies that Bus* (The Dukes Theatre); *Into our Skies* (Lucy Starkey Dance) and *The Box* (Hawkdance Theatre). He's also composed original live scores for silent films *Metropolis*, *Nosferatu* and *The Passion of Joan of Arc*.

2022 sees Lee working on The Theatre Centre and Sheffield Theatre's co-production of *Human Nurture*; The Bare Project's *People's Palace of Possibility* and *Hinterlands*; Jamal Gerald's *Jumbie* and Thick Skin's *Blood Harmony*.

Akeim Toussaint Buck | Movement Director

Akeim Toussaint Buck is an interdisciplinary performer and maker, born in Jamaica and raised in England. Akeim's intention is to create moving, thought provoking, accessible and free-spirited projects. The work challenges, enlightens and entertains in a visceral way, calling on multiple art forms to tell the story. Audiences are invited to not just observe, they are implicit in the experience. His work aims to reflect on reality, looking at ongoing socio-political issues, with a humanitarian intention.

Since graduating from the Northern School of Contemporary Dance with a bachelor's degree in Performing Arts, Akeim has been involved in multiple cross-disciplinary programmes with a wide range of artists and communities from around the world. The aesthetic of his work combines: dance, creative writing, film, poetry, beat-box, singing and acting, fused to tell stories capable of bridging the gaps between a variety of audiences.

Recent achievements include becoming Irie Dance Theatre's Artist-in-Residence for 2019–2020, becoming the Artist for Northern School of Contemporary Dance, Yorkshire Dance and Spin Arts' Catapult 2019. Thanks to Deda Theatre in Derby where Akeim has been recently appointed Associate Artist 2020–2021, gaining more support in his work. Thanks to Geraldine Connor Foundation where Akeim is an Associate Artist. Attaining a Seed Commission for piloting Beatmotion Mass for Leeds Year of Culture 2023. Akeim's work has been supported by Yorkshire Dance, Leeds Playhouse, Leeds Inspired, IRIE! Dance Theatre, Spin Arts, Serendipity, NSCD, Sadler's Wells and Arts Council England. His choreographic work includes: Snakebox's *PLAY*; *Windows of Displacement*; *Reckoning*; *Sib Y Osis*; *Beatmotion*; *Souls & Cells* etc. Film work includes *Galvanise* and *Displaced*.

Lilac Yosiphon | Movement Director

Lilac is a freelance theatre-maker and the artistic director of Althea Theatre. She is passionate about ensemble work, devising and interdisciplinary collaborations. Her practice explores intersectional representation focusing on themes of belonging, migration and our perception of home. She was previously endorsed by Arts Council England as a promising Exceptional Talent in the UK. She is an MGCFutures Bursary recipient and was a finalist for the JMK Award 2019 and Peter Hall 2021.

Previous movement direction and consultancy includes: *Swimming* (The White Bear); *The Indecent Musings of Miss Doncaster 2007* (Camden People's Theatre) and *How Far Apart* (Utopia Theatre).

She is an MGCFutures Bursary recipient and a commissioned artist by Unlimited in partnership with Polka Theatre. She was a finalist for the JMK Award 2019 and the Peter Hall Award 2021.

As a freelance director, she has directed and facilitated workshops for Graeae, Mountview, Guildhall and National Youth Theatre.

Hannah Crossland-Birtswistle | Stage Manager
Training: RADA

Theatre credits include: *Dear Evan Hanson* (Noël Coward Theatre); *Amélie The Musical* (Criterion Theatre); *Harry Potter and the Cursed Child* (Palace Theatre); *42nd Street* (Theatre Royal Drury Lane); *A Midsummer Night's Dream* (The Bridge Theatre); *The Importance of Being Earnest* (The Octagon Theatre); *To Gillie with Love* (Gillian Lynne Theatre); *Show Boat* (New London Theatre); *Lucia de Lammermoor* (Royal Opera House) and *Fantasia: Sounds & Sorcery* (The Vaults, London).

For Sheffield Theatres: *Close Quarters, hang, Standing at the Sky's Edge.*

Victoria Klays | Tour Manager
Tori is a stage manager, movement director and actor from York, now based in Sheffield.

After graduating from The University of Sheffield, Tori has worked across a variety of different roles within the industry. She is passionate about theatre that invites an audience to experience a new and alternative reality, strongly believing that the telling of these stories should be made accessible to all.

Recent stage manager credits include: *My Name is Rachel Corrie* (Theatre Deli); *Neverland* (Theatre Deli and The Vaults).

Recent movement director credits include: *Happiness Engineers* (The Barbican Centre); *The Tempest, Twelfth Night, Hamlet* (Shakespeare's Rose Theatre, York). As assistant movement director: *Beauty and the Beast* (Northumberland Theatre Company).

Recent acting credits include: *The Importance of Being Earnest, Alice in Wonderland, The Little Maid Who Danced to Every Mood* (Northumberland Theatre Company); *The Great Gatsby* (The Guild of Misrule); *The Famous Five, Robin Hood* (Gobbledigook Theatre).

Smart Banda | Artwork & Photography
Smart is a visual communicator and a digital director with over seven years of experience in the creative industry. He specialises in managing digital campaigns and platforms. Smart works with stakeholders, creatives and development teams to deliver digital experiences, websites, and tailored content to promote events and exciting initiatives.

Gomolemo Nyakale | Videographer
Gomolemo (or Goms) is a South African born filmmaker based in the north of the UK. Since graduating in Leeds, Gomolemo has worked on developing his creative style through a range of film projects as well as expanding his skillset in motion graphics, 3D animation, design and photography. His body of work includes: *Gateway East* (director & writer); *One by Jessica Lewis* fashion film (creator & director); *Roof of the World* mini-series (director & Editor); Michael Bird's *Nature* official music video (creator & editor); *Little Sin* short film (editor & camera assistant, and Hope for Justice's *Hrabin's Story* (Director) .
Gomolemo is currently working with independent creators and social activism organisations across the UK to produce exceptional and uniquely compelling work while actively contributing to the betterment of society and communities.

About Roots Mbili Theatre

Roots Mbili Theatre is a Dramatic Arts Production Company specialising in cross-cultural collaborative practice.

Our primary vision is to draw a correlation between the UK and East African theatre industry. We achieve this through education, facilitation and producing work through a collaborative process, bringing together artists with contrasting cultural heritage.

A large branch of Roots Mbili's work is platforming stories from Africa and about African diaspora in the UK, merging culturally distinct storytelling styles in order to create unique and challenging theatre which will have an enduring impact on audiences from both cultures and create creative pathways and exchanges for organisations in their respective countries.

Far Gone is Roots Mbili Theatre's inaugural production.

The Team

Artistic Director	John Rwothomack
Producer	Sam Holland
Digital Director	Smart Banda

About Sheffield Theatres

Sheffield Theatres is home to three theatres: the Crucible, the Sheffield landmark with a world-famous reputation; the Studio, an intimate, versatile space for getting closer to the action; and the gleaming Lyceum, the beautiful proscenium that hosts the best of the UK's touring shows. Committed to investing in the creative leaders of the future, Sheffield Theatres' dedicated talent development hub, The Bank, opened in 2019 to support a new cohort of emerging directors, writers and producers every year. In November 2021, the Crucible and Studio theatres celebrated their 50th anniversary. An anniversary season of work was announced to mark the occasion, including Chris Bush's bold new trilogy *Rock/Paper/Scissors* to be performed across all three venues, plus the highly-anticipated return of Sheffield-set musical *Standing at the Sky's Edge*.

Sheffield Theatres held the title 'Regional Theatre of the Year' for 2020, having previously held the title on an unprecedented three separate occasions. The company has a reputation for bold new work, and over the last year has produced new musical *Standing at the Sky's Edge*, with music and lyrics by Mercury Prize nominated Richard Hawley. The production won the 2020 South Bank Sky Arts Award for theatre and was named Best Musical Production at the 2019 UK Theatre Awards. *Standing at the Sky's Edge* was followed by a dazzling new adaptation of *Life of Pi*, which won four awards at the 2019 UK Theatre Awards, Achievement in Technical Theatre at the Stage Awards and Best New Play at the WhatsOnStage Awards. This success follows the phenomenal Sheffield musical *Everybody's Talking About Jamie* which started life at the Crucible in February 2017, before transferring to the West End later that year. In 2021 the show will resume a UK tour revisiting the Lyceum Theatre in Sheffield in 2022, and the highly anticipated *Everybody's Talking About Jamie* feature film was released simultaneously to 244 countries on Amazon Prime on 17 September 2021.

Crucible Lyceum Studio
55 Norfolk Street, Sheffield, S1 1DA

Joseph Kony and the LRA

The mid-to-late 1980s was a time of political turmoil in Uganda, particularly in the sub-region of Acholiland in the north, near the border with Sudan. Following the removal from power of Idi Amin in 1979, the country's first free and full elections took place in late 1980 and saw former leader Milton Obote (the man Amin seized power from) become President for the second time. His election was contentious, however, with widespread accusations of vote-rigging and voter suppression, and various rebel groups remained at large who did not recognise his Presidency, including the National Resistance Army headed by Yoweri Museveni.

As the second Obote regime took power, Museveni and his NRA continued to wage a rebel bush war, scattering into rural areas and proving difficult to fight against effectively. Despite this, Obote remained President until mid-1985, when the army Commander Tito Okello, frustrated at what he felt was a tribal bias from Obote, seized power through another military coup. Okello immediately sought to engage in peace talks with rebel groups, including Museveni and his NRA, who even signed final treaties with him in late 1985. However, while these talks were ongoing, Museveni had been secretly plotting an assault on Kampala, which he enacted in early 1986, overthrowing Okello and finally seizing power himself. Museveni remains President to this day.

Further into 1986, as Museveni consolidated his rule, he pushed any remaining resistance forces loyal to Okello further north into Acholiland, attempting to disarm the local population as they did so. This met with resistance from a suspicious local population (who had been brutally treated by the Amin regime when they were disarmed in 1971) which in turn led to violent reprisals. This infliction of violence on local people led to greater resentment of Museveni's forces, and eventually a new rebel group was formed, a combination of vengeful local civilians and the remains of Okello's troops, called the Uganda People's Democratic Army. This new UPDA adopted similar tactics to Museveni's own NRA, spreading into rural areas and using guerrilla tactics in another bush war.

As effective as these tactics were, the repercussions were severe for local civilian populations, whose homes and businesses became the main battlegrounds and whose livelihoods were threatened, as they were often perceived to be sheltering the enemy. This instability in northern Uganda continued into early 1987, when the toll taken on local communities started to show, and the UPDA lost support, splintering into smaller disorganised factions, partly due to not having a recognised singular leader. In the wake of their disintegration, yet another rebel group was formed, this time led by a woman called Alice Auma, called the Holy Spirit Movement.

Auma distinguished her group by being explicitly religious, presenting herself as a spiritual medium who was channelling a Christian Holy Spirit called 'Lakwena'. This galvanised almost all remaining resistance to Museveni, and Auma's HSM was very successful, pursuing government forces out of Acholiland and pushing further south, hoping to take Kampala and overthrow Museveni himself. They were met with severe government defences further south, however, and were eventually defeated near Jinja, their main army routed, and Auma fled east to Kenya. While she was pursuing this assault further south, the power vacuum back north in Acholiland was filled by a man reported to be her cousin Joseph Kony.

Using very similar quasi-religious justification to Auma, Kony established a Christian fundamentalist theocratic movement in northern Uganda, using the same tactics as Museveni himself had used with his NRA, the same guerrilla warfare approach of the UPDA, and the same bush war ideology of Auma's HSM – his army was even initially called HSM2. After changing its name to the Lord's Salvation Army, he declared himself the spokesperson of God and through a system of child-soldier abduction and religious terrorism established a firm grip on Acholiland. By the early 1990s his group had become known as the Lord's Resistance Army, continuing its rebellion in northern Uganda, and Kony remains at large to this day, though his whereabouts are unknown and his influence has greatly diminished.

A Word or Two from the Writer

As a little boy, aged eight, I was nearly kidnapped by the rebel group the Lords Resistance Army (LRA), led by the notorious Joseph Kony, from my home in a northern Ugandan village. Ten years later, now not so little, I was in my first year of drama school and was stunned to see a video by Invisible Children, an American NGO calling for the capture of Joseph Kony. The video entitled 'Kony 2012' becomes a viral phenomenon, except that it comes far, far too late. Inspired to take back the narrative, it was at that point the idea for the play was conceived. Some years later, *Far Gone* was written, came to life and now you're reading this.

This play is not about me, the kid who was lucky enough to escape. This play is for the hundreds of thousands who did not. For the parents whose children were either lost forever or forever changed. For the girls who were forced into child marriage to men old enough to be their fathers. For the brothers, sisters, cousins, nieces, nephews, sons and daughters who lost the innocence of childhood, simply for being born at an unfortunate time in an unfortunate geographical location. For the future generations who will continue to suffer the trauma the LRA has marked on them for many years to come.

For you all.

John Rwothomack

FAR GONE

John Rwothomack

'When the missionaries came to Africa they had the Bible
and we had the land. They said "Let us pray."
We closed our eyes. When we opened them we had
the Bible and they had the land.'

Desmond Tutu

4

Characters

OKUMU
OKELLO, *his brother*
COMMANDANT
SPRINKLER

This play was originally performed as a one-man show.

We move between Northern Uganda and Juba, South Sudan.

This text went to press before the end of rehearsals and so may differ slightly from the play as performed.

As we enter, OKUMU *is playing udhilu, a game of 'spin the wood'. The game involves tying a piece of string around a piece of wood and then spinning it on the floor. As the piece of wood spins, it is hit with the piece of string to keep it spinning. He will invite audience members to join him in the game, where they can't play he will endeavour to teach them.*

OKUMU (*to one audience member*). Hello, if I invited you to come with me on a journey, a story, will you come with me? Thank you!

He gives the piece of wood to the audience member.

Hey, hello, what about you? Sir/madam, if I welcomed you to listen to a story, my story? Will you lend me your ears? Thank you.

He give the piece of string to this audience member.

Hello, thank you all, thank you for coming. I have a story to tell, it is very important to me, will you favour me with your eyes and ears and voices? Yes? Thank you, thank you...

Your eyes will see, your ears will hear, but your voices I am going to need them. There's a man you are going to meet, the commandant. He is going to need you to answer some of his questions when he asks you. It is not hard, let us try. For example, when the commandant says...

COMMANDANT. De commandant is feeling very generous today.

OKUMU. He will then ask you...

COMMANDANT. How does de commandant feel?

OKUMU. Your answer...?

He waits for us to answer, this will be repeated twice. The COMMANDANT *might correct the audience to answer 'very generous' if they only answer with 'generous'.*

And if he says…

COMMANDANT. De commandant has changed his mind. What has de commandant done?

The COMMANDANT *waits for the audience to answer.*

What has de commandant done?

Again, waits for the audience to answer.

We are called the Lord's Resistance Army. What are we called?

He waits for us to answer.

What are we called?

Waits again.

After the audience answer, he leads them in a chant.

LRA! LRA! LRA!

OKUMU. My name is Okumu. I am from Minakulu village, in Lira in the north of Uganda. My mother – (*Taking out a picture.*) Alice Adong, she is the best. She cooks for me the okra and fish when I am not feeling very well. My father, Agama David, he is a farmer, everybody says he is a good man, but he is always beating me and my brother. I have two older brothers, but my parents said when I was two years old Vincent Opio, the eldest, was sent away – well, disowned by my father. The story begins when me and my other brother, Okello, were playing outside.

OKELLO. Okumu, are you going to play it properly today?

OKELLO *starts the spin the wood game as we saw* OKUMU *playing at the beginning of the play but it is mimed this time. He sets it up for* OKUMU, *who hits the wood and stops it from rotating, and so stopping the game.*

OKUMU. I'm sorry, Okello, I'm sorry.

(*To us.*) My brother, even though he is only two years older than me, he is so much bigger and stronger and better than me in anything physical. But up here, God did not bless him, even a goat is better than him. Don't laugh, he is my brother. He also has a very bad temper.

OKUMU *hands back the stick to* OKELLO, *who re-starts the game, hands the stick to* OKUMU – *who fails again.*

OKELLO. Okumu! Use the string, not the stick! One more and I am going to kill you.

OKELLO *resets the game for the second time for* OKUMU, *who fails again.*

OKUMU. Okello, I am sorry, I am sorry… no… no…

He runs as OKELLO *is chasing him. The boys chase each other.* OKELLO *eventually reaches* OKUMU. *He goes to grab him, but he misses as* OKUMU *dodges him.*

Haha… haha… you missed me, you missed!

OKELLO. You come here!

OKELLO *grabs* OKUMU*'s leg and pulls* OKUMU *towards him.*

OKUMU. No no… no leave me alone.

OKELLO *begins tickling* OKUMU.

No… no… no don't tickle me…

Hahahahahha… no… no… hahha… no.

OKELLO. Ehh, eh, what are you saying now… eh? Eh? You idiot. Look at you.

As the boys continue play-fighting we hear two sounds of gunshots in the distance. They freeze.

OKUMU. Did you hear that?

OKELLO. Yes…

Silence.

Pause.

Rapid gunshots are heard followed by people screaming, shouting and running from rebels.

GET UP! GET UP! RUN! Come, come!

OKELLO *beckons* OKUMU *to follow, they find a place to hide behind the bushes.* OKELLO *may peep to see what's going on.* OKUMU *is scared on the ground. He speaks to us.*

OKUMU. The Lord's Resistance Army, LRA, the rebels. They always stopped in nearby villages, never came to our village, but this time they made it. (*Standing up.*) We hid behind the bushes, far away from the village and we waited for a long time. It was chaos, a lot of noises, bullets, children screaming, mothers running with their babies. And the men, they were just running, they didn't know what to do. My uncle, I have never seen a man cry like that. I covered my ears, but it was impossible, the noise it was too much, it pierced through my bones.

(*Getting back in position.*) We waited, we waited till the sound died and the rebels left.

OKELLO *peeps to assess the situation. He is happy for them to come out of hiding and he beckons* OKUMU, *who is still in shock and slacking behind, to follow him. As they make their way back to the village, they see their parents' corpses on the floor. As they mourn, they are attacked by* SPRINKLER, *a rebel who has stayed behind just in case such a situation arose.*

Papa, Mama…

SPRINKLER (*speaking Luo and sometimes Swahili*). Anonku wuu, u ringu ungo. Kujapa, kujapa, wenani. [I found you, you're not gonna run away. Come here, come here.]

Between this he has kicked both OKUMU *and* OKELLO *to their knees, he calls for the* COMMANDANT.

Commandant! Commandant! U ki too…! U too…! [You are gonna die today.]

COMMANDANT. Sprinkler, wello done, wello done! Tonight, you shall be rewarded with one of de virgins! Now, what rats do we have here? Dis one is strong eh, but dis one, can dis one even be a soldier? It is weak. Sprinkler, de commandant is feeling very generous today – How does de commandant feel?

Awaits audience's reply, he will repeat the question until they answer.

I want to see da Sprinkler in action.

(*Pointing to* OKUMU.) So why don't you get rid of dis little rat?

SPRINKLER. Commandant. Afoyo. [Thank you.]

He goes to shoot OKUMU. OKELLO *in a very swift move rugby-tackles* SPRINKLER *to the ground and starts throwing punches at him. In the struggle between the two* SPRINKLER *pulls out a knife and stabs* OKELLO *in the stomach.* OKUMU *is on the floor crying and mumbling his brother's name.* OKELLO *is grabbed and dragged by other soldiers.* SPRINKLER *jumps to his feet, grabs the knife and is ready to finish* OKELLO. *Just before the knife reaches* OKELLO, *the* COMMANDANT *interrupts.*

COMMANDANT. Wait! De commandant has changed his mind – What has de commandant done?

Awaits audience's response and then points to OKUMU.

Let us see if dis little rat can be a soldier.

He walks to OKUMU.

Nyingi ngha? [What's your name?] Okumu. So Okumu, jal eh – [This one] what is he to you? Eh? Why is he willing to die for you? Speak! Ahh... now you see, Okumu, your brother here, he have done a very stupid thing and mek Sprinkler here very angry, so he going to have to be dying... but for you, Okumu, you are very lucky today, because today, de commandant is feeling very generous – How does de commandant feel?

If there's a little hesitation from the audience he may be angered.

So, it is up to you to choose if you live or you die. Sprinkler, give me de knife. You see dis one is a knife and here is de heart, and you stab it hard once, any man will die. Come.

OKUMU *takes the knife but is very hesitant to stab his brother.*

Do it! Sprinkler, how is your gun? Do you want to sprinkle some bullets in de air?

The COMMANDANT *watches the bullets go in the air.*

Do you want Sprinkler to sprinkle dos bullets in you?

OKUMU *stabs* OKELLO, *but it's weak a stab.*

Again! Again! Again!

The boy repeats the actions as the COMMANDANT *shouts at him.* OKELLO *is stabbed to death, his body lays on the floor and slowly he transforms into* OKUMU *in a fetal position, crying for his brother.*

OKUMU. My brother… my brother… my brother…

The mourning turns into a physical movement which will continue through the voice-over of the 'White Man' poem. It is as if OKUMU *has been possessed by some power he is trying to get rid of – an exorcism.*

'White Man':

VOICE-OVER.
  White man, come and teach me your civilised culture.
  White man, come and educate me on your beautiful
    language.
  White man, come and impregnate me with your faultless
    religion.
  Oh white man, come, come and walk me through the
    principles of living a good life.

  Come, oh come, dearest white man.
  I invite you into the comfort of my hut,

Come and teach our politicians the democracy of power.
Come, white man, come hold my hands and guide my fingers
   on the etiquette of writing history.

Oh come into my house and afford me the respect of naming
   my national resources after your kings and queens, princes
   and princesses.

Nalubaale – Victoria
Rutanzige – Edward
Mwitanzige – Albert
Dweru – George

Now that my land floors with your vernacular and my mind
   reads your language,
Teach me the sacred meanings of the scriptures of your holy
   book.
How those very words contradict.
Nurture me in using the same book to preach peace and with
   the next page stimulate a war.
Teach me, white man, oh teach me.
Rip another verse out of that page and lead me through
   journey of obedience.
From king to slave.

And now help me distinguish between black and white.
How with white comes independence, freedom and birthright.
With black the entanglement of persecution and oppression.
Oh you can't go yet, white man.
You haven't yet taught me the greatest art of them all.
Teach me how to hate my brother.
Train my mind how best to capture his children and sell them
   to you.
Oh teach me how to go to war with him.

Not with these ancient spears, bows and arrows my ancestors
   used.
But with these bullet-firing metals you gave me in exchange.
In exchange for my brother's children.

Now that the transformation is done,
Be gone and let us kill one another.

OKUMU. I was no longer a child, I was a boy who killed his brother… I am a Luo, in Luo we must bid farewell to the dead and let their spirits be free or else they will just wander and never rest. I must set his spirit free.

OKUMU *is in tears as he goes to* OKELLO*'s corpse to say a traditional farewell. As he starts to do the ritual he is pulled back by* SPRINKLER.

SPRINKLER. Itimu angony? Ay malu! [What are you doing? Get up!]

OKUMU. No no no… let me say goodbye, let me set his spirit free. I must say… I have to… Okello… Okello…

SPRINKLER *yanks* OKUMU, *pulling him back.* OKUMU *continues mumbling and crying, making* SPRINKLER *grow more and more impatient and irritated.*

SPRINKLER. SHUT UP! Commandant, anege. [Commandant, I'm gonna kill him.]

COMMANDANT (*calming* SPRINKLER *down and going to* OKUMU). My boy, you are now a kurut, LRA. And LRA have rules. Rule number acel [one]: LRA don't cry. Number ario [two]: de dead are de dead. Oh, and dis one, dis one is a very special one, because it only for you. If you continue to crying, you will join de dead.

OKUMU *stops crying.*

Good. Sprinkler, the bag of maize, that bag of maize, load him. Now!

A heavy load of food that has just been looted is loaded on OKUMU*'s back. The load is heavy enough to be too heavy for a fully grown man.* OKUMU *almost falls backwards due to the heaviness of the load. When the* COMMANDANT *feels everybody is ready enough to his satisfaction, he blows his whistle to mark the beginning of the march.* OKUMU*'s walk starts with big steps which get smaller with time. We should see the effects of the long walk: a fly might land on him, the thickness of the forest, his awareness of everyone around him, etc…*

The march continues for as long as is appropriate. OKUMU
*is in pain from the march, he is aching all over his body, all
the energy is draining out him as he slowly settles down,
taking off his luggage to rest for the night.*

OKUMU. It has been five days of walking all day and only
resting at night. For two nights, no food, ah, what will I do?
How will I survive this bush? I am clever, but I am not clever
for the bush. I like books, I read books. My favourite book is
Black Beauty. The one about the horse. I am not strong. For a
week my head is thinking about my brother... my mother
where are... my father... my brother... I try to pray... Maria
ma leng ni mungu... [Hail Mary full of grace...]

*As he sleeps, we see him having a bad dream. He's startled
by the dream and wakes himself up. In front of him is a
spotlight symbolising* OKELLO*'s* GHOST.

Okello... is that you? No, no, no, no... you are dead!

*He wakes up. He closes his eyes in the hope that he is
dreaming. He opens them and the* GHOST *is still there.*

No, no, no... is this a dream?!

Getting up.

It was a dark night, everybody was sleeping, the forest was
making noise, the trees, the owls, but he was here, I could
see him, I could hear him, I could touch...

He goes to touch the GHOST *but his hands pass through it.*

Who are you, what are you?

GHOST. Okumu, it is okay, it is me, Okello, your brother. Don't
be scared, Okumu, if you scream, they will think you are
crazy. They cannot see or hear me. It is okay. Come, give me
your hand. It is okay.

The GHOST *gives* OKUMU *his hand.* OKUMU *tries to hold
the* GHOST*'s hand but physical contact is impossible.*

OKUMU. I cannot touch you, why?

GHOST. Come, let us sit down.

OKUMU. I am sorry... I am so sorry... I...

GHOST. Okumu, it is okay, I wanted you to do it. If you did not do it, you also would be dead. You did the right thing. It is that Sprinkler...

OKUMU. I killed my brother...

GHOST. No, no, you saved your life. Say it.

OKUMU *is silent*.

Okumu, say it.

OKUMU. I saved my life.

Pause.

The GHOST *takes a good look at* OKUMU.

GHOST. You remember when I told you I would die before I let anything happen to you? Well I am dead now, hahahaha.

OKUMU. That is not funny!

GHOST. Yes, you are right. Sorry. Okumu, you must snap out of it, eh, or you're not going to survive. You have to be better, you have to be stronger, I did not die so that you come here and be baby, you have to survive this place and carry the family name.

OKUMU. It is hard, Okello.

GHOST. I know, brother, but your big brother is here.

OKUMU (*starts to do the ritual to set his brother free – he does the full ritual*). You are dead. Your spirit should be resting. Not here.

OKUMU *does the burial ritual again, but this time it's much faster and clumsy.*

GHOST. Okumu, stop, stop, you can't send me to rest, not like this.

OKUMU. But how?

GHOST. I have told you, that Sprink/ler...

We hear a high-pitched scream in the distance.

COMMANDANT. Dey have finded her. Sprinkler, bring her here. Untie dis, dat one, give him de machete, dis rat here give her a stone, dis stupid mosquito, give her another machete…

He looks at OKUMU, *pauses for a short while, then changes his mind.*

Ahh, Okumu, you must watch. Sprinkler, and dat rat, give him de knife.

Pause.

(*To us.*) Do you want de commandant to be generous? (*He waits for the answer.*) No, not today, you cannot be generous to anybody who tries to escape. Even if she is a potential wife of Lapony Ladit. Hehehe ahh, Lapony Ladit, Joseph Kony he have many wives eh… hehe… Now for all of you new kuruts, dey are certain things to needi to understandi. Dis war that we are fighting, we are fighting in the name of the Lord. God. De heavenly Father. De holy spirit, Lakwena dat chosed to come to Joseph Kony, Lapony Ladit, our master, is a holy spirit from God. And in de name of God, we are going to be to be winning dis war. We are going to be to be what?

Awaits audience response.

And dat is why we are called the Lord's Resistance Army. What are we called?

Awaits audience response.

What are we called?

The chant will turn into a song led by the COMMANDANT.

˙Pe tye gin maloyo Rubanga, aleluya
Lweny bene walwenyo I nyinge, aleluya.

[There is nothing that defeats God,
This war we are fighting in his name, hallelujah.]

And who here does not believe in God? Good. In the holy book, what does God do to the people of Sodom and Gomorrah that disobey him? Hmm?

Awaits audience response, room for improvisation depending on the audience's answers. He can say 'well done, etc.' to an audience member who answers correctly.

So if you try to escape you disobey de commandant, and if you disobey de commandant, you disobey de… Lord's Resistance Army…

He starts chanting 'LRA!' and encourages us to join.

Okay, okay, shut up!

Signalling us to stop chanting.

…and if you disobey de LRA you disobey… God and if you disobey God you must… die.

He signals the four kuruts to start hacking at the escapee, as the song continues. At first, she screams, begging them to stop and asking what she had done to them, but the four kids are somehow energised and overtaken by the chant and words of the COMMANDANT *and it doesn't help that they are at gunpoint.We turn to* OKUMU *and the* GHOST *who have been spectators to the whole thing.* OKUMU, *however, hasn't joined in with the chant and is trying to look away from the scene.*

GHOST. Okumu, if you are going to survive you must now become like them. You must now be strong. You must watch. And don't cry.

OKUMU (*tries his best to hold himself together but he simply can't*). I can… I can't… I cannot… this is…

GHOST. Oku… don't cr… stop crying. Okumu, do you want to die?! The commandant is watching you.

OKUMU. I cannot, Okello, I cannot.

GHOST. Okay, okay, it's okay. Look at me. Look at me. Keep your eyes on me. Don't look away. I am going to stand there…

Pointing in the direction of the scene.

Just look at me.

He walks backwards towards the direction of the scene, keeping eye contact with OKUMU at all times.

Okumu, stay with me. Good. Stop crying. Now wipe your tears. Good. Now look at her. Keep looking. Good, breathe, brother, breathe.

Once he is satisfied that OKUMU can look at the girl's dead body by himself, he walks back to OKUMU. OKUMU is staring at the direction of the scene. We see a little change in him, an acceptance that he is no longer a little boy but an LRA kurut.

OKUMU (*to us*). Even though I cannot touch him, I can see him. I can hear him, and I know he is here with me. I know I have to be better. I have to be stronger. Stronger. I have to set him free. So the next day I try harder, I walk faster, the load is still heavy but it feels a little bit lighter. He is here, with me, next to me, walking with me. MY BROTHER! And now I have hope. I know I can survive this bush.

In Juba, in Sudan, we finally reached the LRA home after four weeks of walking. There are so many children here, in my heart I want to go to them and play a game of... but I get the feeling there is no playing here. Most of the children have guns, everybody has a panga. They look like the tooth fairy came and stole away their smile.

For the next week we did training.

SPRINKLER. Aya, aya uu bin, wa ki timu training. [Alright, alright, gather around, everyone, we are going start training.]

SPRINKLER calls for a kurut to approach him. He runs the kurut through the process of holding a wooden gun, SPRINKLER helps him get in a posture and position. He is tough but fair. The process is repeated with another kurut, of a different height. SPRINKLER looks for OKUMU, he calls him forward with a lot more force and aggression than he used on the first two kuruts. OKUMU is scared and can't move.

SPRINKLER *goes to him, grabs him by the neck and arms, forces him into the position. Hands him the wooden gun. SPRINKLER slaps* OKUMU *on the head. Loses his patience, grabs* OKUMU *by the head again and pushes him on the floor.* SPRINKLER *begins whipping* OKUMU. *On the third whip,* SPRINKLER *turns into* OKUMU. *We see* OKUMU *being whipped three times. On the third stroke he slowly gets up and turns into the* GHOST.

GHOST. Okumu, ey – (*Clicking his fingers.*) C'mon, get up. Remember you need to survive eh. You are stronger than that, brother.

OKUMU *gets into another position, we see a change in him from the frigid little boy to a kid who is starting to ever so slightly master the training process. We see him in three different positions. By the time he gets to the third, he is a much better-trained soldier. Towards the end of the training sequence the* COMMANDANT, *who has been watching from a distance, appears.*

COMMANDANT. Okumu, I have been watching you, you are doing very well. Sprinkler, well done. Get me my Suzan. Harry up, run! (*To* OKUMU.) Throw away dat wooden piece of wood. Let me introduce you to Suzan, she is from Russia. She was de first for me. Now if you are going to stop to be to be being a kurut and become holie, a soldier, you are going have to be to be learning to how to shoot.

The COMMANDANT *walks* OKUMU *through the process of shooting a gun.*

Now listen properly. Dis is de magazine. You push de bullets into it like dis... but we are not going to be using de bullets today, dey are too expensive. Don't worry, you are going to be using dem when it matters. Now, you hold de magazine like dis, rotate it back and lock into de gun like this. And den pull dis ting on de right like dis. And you are ready. Here.

You are going to be to be having to be giving her back, you are going to be having to be earning your own gun.

OKUMU. The final drill was 'Cordon and Destroy', but now
I have a gun. And I can go on missions.

*As 'Cordon and Destroy' is acted out, it turns from a training
session to a real-life situation where* OKUMU, SPRINKLER
and the COMMANDANT *end up on a mission to 'Cordon
and Destroy' two Ugandan soldiers.*

Two Ugandan soldiers. They were just there, they looked
like they were lost.

COMMANDANT. Okay, okay, we are going to 'Cordon and
Destroy' dem. Sprinkler, take de right, over dere, Killa you
too, Damager dere. Okumu –

He signals OKUMU *to take the left.*

Ready? Aya, acel, ario... [Okay, one, two...]

We see OKUMU *in the position the* COMMANDANT
appointed him to. We hear a single gunshot.

OKUMU (*to us*). The Commandant shot one dead.

Pause.

Another shot is fired.

(*To us.*) Sprinkler shot the other one on the leg, he was about
to sprinkle him.

(*To the* COMMANDANT.) Commandant, let me do it. Let
me do it.

OKUMU *goes to the injured soldier, points his gun to his
head, but he can't get himself to finish the job.*

Okello...

GHOST. Hello, little brother. Look at him, look carefully, if you
don't kill him, you die. Now aim higher, to the head. All you
have to do is pull.

OKUMU *fires at the Ugandan soldier's head. The force of
the shot sends him back a bit. He is still.*

COMMANDANT. Okumu, wello done, wello done. You have finished him. FINISHER!!!

OKUMU (*to us*). In that moment three things happened; I earned my own gun, the commandant trusted me and I lost my name. I am now a holie and holies have new names. I was now Finisher.

The first time you kill by choice, it is hard, but then it gets easier, it becomes the way of life, like… breathing air. Three months: if you see a Ugandan soldier, you better finish him before he finishes you. (*To* GHOST.) Brother, I will release you. (*To us*.) Eight months: you have to eat, so you attack the villages and find food. And if there's someone in the village who will not give their food, you ask politely with a gun. (*To* GHOST.) Brother, he is still too powerful, when I'm ready, I will release you. You will be free. (*To us*.) Two years: and the commandant gives you the order to chop off the lips, or ears or noses or tongues… I have to survive. (*To* GHOST.) Brother, I will release you. I will get him, I promise.

Brother, you keep talking about surviving this place, but if I survive, and I free you, where will I go?

GHOST. Okumu, you cannot be thinking like that, look at this place.

OKUMU. You are right, it is not a good place. For a civilian. But I am not a kurut any more, I am a soldier, a holie, and like Lapony Ladit Joseph Kony said, there's a specific place in heaven for soldiers, because soldiers have to do things that civilians cannot do, God will judge me differently.

GHOST. Let me remind you who you are. You are not 'Finisher', you are Okumu Laurence, from Minakulu. My brother.

OKUMU. You are dead.

GHOST. Son of David Agama and your mother is Alice Adong.

OKUMU. Was.

GHOST. Okay, your elder brother Vincent Opio, he is still alive.

OKUMU. You don't know if that is true, and I don't even know him.

GHOST. Okumu.

OKUMU. What?

GHOST. You are different.

OKUMU. I am a holie.

GHOST. Okay, okay, I need to be free, will you do that for me? Will you finish that Sprinkler?

OKUMU. Three years: and I have become good at being a soldier. (*To* GHOST.) Brother, you are almost free. He is not junior commandant any more. (*To us.*) Five years; and I am now junior commandant. (*To* GHOST.) Brother, Sprinkler is now under my command. And I know how much the commandant loves his honey.

COMMANDANT. Everybody, gader around! Gader around! Everybody gader around now! Finisher, get dem, get everybody here! Get dem! Bring dem!

(*To us.*) De commandant is very angry. De commandant is what?

Awaits a reply, but he cuts the audience before they finish answering.

De commandant is what?

He now addresses both the audience and the holies gathered around as one.

There is a thief here, there is a thief among you and we are going to be finding who dey are today. We are de LRA, and de LRA do not steal. I am going to be to be giving you de chance to be speaking right now, if you are de one who stole my honey.

Pause.

He waits for a reply.

No one. Finisher, come forward.

OKUMU. Commandant, lapony, I am sorry that somebody stole you honey. And forgive me for speaking, commandant, but I think it would be a very good idea to search everybody's bag, and see, maybe we will find the honey. We are the LRA and LRA do not steal. We have to be to be being better. Let us just search the bags eh.

COMMANDANT. Errr, Finisher, you are going to be to be making a fine commandant one day. Very good. Search de bags.

OKUMU (*to a holie*). Inn [you], bring you bag here.

He empties the first bag, there is no sign of the honey.

You stupid, show me.

He empties another bag, there is no sign of the honey.

Sprinkler, let me see yours.

He empties SPRINKLER's *bag with more aggression and anger. The honey falls out of the bag.* OKUMU *picks it up, stares at* SPRINKLER.

SPRINKLER. Commandant, ebe volu. Ubedu an ngo. Aja kwo ngo. [Commandant, it's a lie, I didn't do it. I am not a thief.]

OKUMU *picks up the honey and goes to give it to the* COMMANDANT, *who signals him to step aside.*

COMMANDANT. Sprinkler…!

Addressing everyone now.

What is de eight commandiment in de bible?

He waits for a reply, he will not continue until he gets it. If there's no answer he can say: de commandant does not like to be repeating himself.

(*Directly at the audience member who answered him.*) Good. Very good. We are de LRA and de LRA obey de commandiments.

SPRINKLER *knows it is over for him. He pleads for the last time to the* COMMANDANT, *but* SPRINKLER *himself knows there's no hope. As he pleads, the holies around start beating and stoning him. He has no choice but to run for his life. As he runs, the* COMMANDANT *takes out his pistol and shoots him in the stomach, the exact place* SPRINKLER *stabbed* OKELLO. SPRINKLER *is on the floor, struggling for his life.*

Finisher, finish him.

OKUMU, *for a moment, looks at the wounded* SPRINKLER *on the floor. He takes out his knife, slowly, stands for a moment, then with a sudden and quick move he stabs* SPRINKLER *with all his might until there's no life left in the body. As he stabs...*

OKUMU. Brother, now you are free. Okello, now you rest. I set you free. I set you free.

Pause.

He wipes the blood from his knife on SPRINKLER*'s dead body.*

COMMANDANT. Get rid of dis thief and take everything from him.

OKUMU *drags* SPRINKLER*'s body by the leg to a secluded place. He takes* SPRINKLER*'s gun, checks if it's still good to use, and places it to the side. He yanks a necklace from* SPRINKLER*'s chest, looks at it and throws it away. He notices a piece of paper hidden in* SPRINKLER*'s inner shorts pocket, he takes it out, and discovers it is a picture of Alice Adong, a copy of the picture he showed us at the beginning of the play. Behind the picture there is a note. He reads it.*

Vincent, my son, my Opio
I am sorry that this has happened to you.
I know you are innocent, but your papa will not listen.
Keep this picture with you.
Remember me by it,

I will never forget you, my son.
You mother, Alice Adong.

OKUMU *is realising who* SPRINKLER *is. He is overcome with the fact he just killed him. He is completely still.*

Silence.

SPRINKLER*'s ghost rises from his dead body and is staring at* OKUMU.

***

Everything's a story, and as such it must end.

A Nick Hern Book

Far Gone first published in Great Britain in 2022 as a paperback original by Nick Hern Books Limited, The Glasshouse, 49a Goldhawk Road, London W12 8QP, in association with Roots Mbili Theatre

Far Gone copyright © 2022 John Rwothomack

John Rwothomack has asserted his right to be identified as the author of this work

Cover image by Smart Banda

Designed and typeset by Nick Hern Books, London
Printed in Great Britain by Mimeo Ltd, Huntingdon, Cambridgeshire PE29 6XX

A CIP catalogue record for this book is available from the British Library

ISBN   978 1 83904 073 3

Woodland
CARBON
www.woodlandcarbon.co.uk
NICK HERN BOOKS
Printed on Carbon Captured paper

www.nickhernbooks.co.uk

facebook.com/nickhernbooks

twitter.com/nickhernbooks